# WOMXN

# WOMXN

*To Len (my beloved husband) and Matt, for striking up a real conversation with a stranger in the park. Look what you've begun! Thank you, thank you, thank you.*

*To my daughters, Marley and Delphi. I hope, like every parent, that you never have these words pointed at you, but if you do, take this book down off the shelf. Most anger directed at you is nothing to do with you at all. But it can hurt. There is healing in here, my loves, and word magic. Keep being exactly you. I love you.*

*To the womxn in my life – old and new, for better or worse, forever or for a spell. Thank you, I'm sorry, please forgive me, I love you …*

An Hachette UK Company
www.hachette.co.uk

First published in Great Britain in 2021 by Pyramid,
a division of Octopus Publishing Group Ltd
Carmelite House, 50 Victoria Embankment, London EC4Y 0DZ
www.octopusbooks.co.uk

Text copyright © Lexy Wren-Sillevis, 2021
Illustrations copyright © Margaux Carpentier, 2021

ISBN 978-0-7537-3453-7

A CIP catalogue record for this book is available from the British Library

Printed and bound in China

10 9 8 7 6 5 4 3 2 1

Publisher: Lucy Pessell
Designer: Hannah Coughlin
Editor: Sarah Kennedy
Editorial Assistant: Emily Martin
Production Controller: Serena Savini

# WOMXN

# STICKS & STONES

## acrostics & poems to reclaim the words that have hurt us

### LEXY WREN-SILLEVIS

#### Illustrated by Margaux Carpentier

# INTRODUCTION

A stranger called me sexy and it completely changed my life. Words can do that. One word, spoken but once – a complete game-changer. Perhaps that sounds familiar, yet also slightly ridiculous. Well, that's life folks, and we live in a very complex world. Here's how it happened for me.

Way back when, I was sitting outside a café with some girlfriends when a man joined us at our table. If he'd been anyone else we'd have stood up and left but he wasn't just anyone else. He hopped off his shiny pink bike and sort of glided over to us and was so un-pedestrian and tanned and, well, extraordinary, that we were all awestruck. (I know, it doesn't take an awful lot to impress us sometimes, does it?) Anyway, he sat down and proceeded to enlighten me and my friends on what he thought of our looks and how they would affect our lives. Yep, straight in there. A big, important, unsolicited life-lesson from a tall-ish, pink-biked stranger.

"Well, you're GORGEOUS," he said to one friend. "Really striking. What a face!" And then to the other friend: "And you're so BEAUTIFUL I could cry. Oh to be that beautiful! Right?" He turned to me. "Oh, well you are neither beautiful nor PRETTY. But (he held his finger up at this point) you are SEXY! And that will work for you." I was crushed. Of course I was. Nevermind the who and why and what, I had just been pronounced to be sexy, but neither beautiful nor pretty. In front of my friends. By someone who had ascended to god-like status simply by having a tan and descending from a saddle. I smiled and swallowed it down, pretending it didn't taste like poison. I bundled it up and put it away.

But putting something away is only ever the thing you do before having to pick it up again. That one word defined the whole of my teens and twenties. I was neither beautiful nor pretty and therefore (or so I thought back then) I must be UGLY. But I was sexy – pink bike man had said so. So from then on, having been branded and packaged with that one single word, I believed the writing on the box. I internalised his edict and behaved accordingly, losing my virginity soon after and spending years thinking that sex – be it good, bad or forgettable sex – was love. Or as close to love as sexy-ugly me was going to get.

Fast forward many years to now, and I have two incredible daughters. I also have two decades of dedication to Healing and using the wisdom of Hindsight behind me. High or tipsy as he might have been, inappropriate and downright weird as he definitely seemed when I came to think of it later, I know man on pink bike was wrong. In every single way.

As the saying goes: "Hurt people hurt people". And it's the words they use that hurt us most. In fact, some words are used so frequently, and so casually – and often by people who say they like, or love, or respect us – that we don't even notice the hurt until some time later. Like jellyfish, these words glide by and only when they're at a distance do we notice the sting of their tentacles. Words cast spells over us. Words are powerful. In safe hands, and from the sweet mouth, they can coax you into your best self, lift your day, ease your fears. Yet in wounded, suffering, punishing hands they can suffocate and hold us under. They slice into our self-esteem and leave a deep, dark wound.

So when a little while ago, my eldest came back from school, saying that another child had called her a BIG FAT PIG, I wanted to make it better. I wanted to spare her what I'd been through. I didn't want her spinning the words BIG and FAT and PIG over and over in her head. I didn't want those words to have even the slightest chance of shaping her life. So I sat and wrote "big fat pig" in large letters and the acrostic wrote itself.

An acrostic is a poem, word puzzle or other composition of words in which certain letters in each line form a word or words. They can be simple and reactionary or loaded with meaning and intention, as I have come to discover. The acrostics in this book are both. They take the words, the slurs, the insults and the labels that are thrown at us and break them down, and tear them apart. This book is a righting of wrongs, a rewriting of the words that diminish us. It transmutes and rewrites those words – some with all of the pain they trigger, others as positive affirmations, mantras and poems.

My daughter and I have added other words to our list: ANNOYING, SNITCH, OVAL HEAD (I mean, really?!) and each time we've written an acrostic it has led us to incredible conversations about being human, being brave, as well as life, hurt, purpose, soul. I began to write down every word that had hurt me or my loved ones, and all too easily I got to sixty words. The former journalist in me wriggled free and I set out on a mission to grow that list into a list of words that are flung at women other than me and mine. Since I began writing, so many women have wanted to share their painful words with me; I've had so many coffees and late-night chats and emails about reclaimed words. And here's the thing. There are so many words. So many insults and labels and boxes for women to be packaged and packed off in. Often, but not always, they're words coined by men. Why that is, is another book, and is a bigger conversation that is starting to be had by women everywhere. We're slowly, but oh-so-surely, making it clear that there is no man in womxn. We're writing him out and writing us back in. Not because we don't love men – they are our divine brothers, fathers, sons, uncles, partners, husbands, friends. But because we are equals and deserve our own term. Our own word with a suffix all of our own. So from here on in we are womxn.

Writing this book has been a huge lesson in a life of them and it has been an incredible and humbling experience. As a colour therapist, energy psychologist, spiritual coach, and womxn, I'd like this book to be a tool for your own transformation, change and healing; you opt in as much as you like. Yes, she's glossy and utterly gorgeous, but she's also a timeless workbook for feminine healing if you need her – to take the sting and hurt and pain out of the words that have hurt you.

I've taken SEXY out of pink bike man's mouth and UGLY out of my very being. My daughter watched BIG FAT PIG become something so very, very different. And she's stronger for it. I won't share BIG FAT PIG here; that one was for my daughter and a gift to her. But the rest are for you.

So here's to taking back your sovereignty, dignity and divinity. Sticks and stones may break your bones but soon these words will never hurt you.

With great warmth,

Lexy x

**YOUR**

**HEALING**

I have learned that everything we encounter has a vibration. Vibration forms everything in life. Colour is a living energy and a property of light, and each colour has its own specific frequency. We can be moved by other energies in our field, so it makes sense that an energy can affect another energy. Colour affects us, just as words and the intention behind them affects us. We must choose to curate a life with the vibrations that bring us joy, healing and peace. Colour helps with that; energy work helps with that. This book helps with that.

As you read through it, let your eyes absorb the colours of Margaux Carpentier's extraordinary illustrations: let the energy of the words go to the wounded places within you. Trust that you are safe there.

Although the choice of words to clear and heal in this book was mine as an author and researcher, the acrostics have always seemed to flow through me. In authoring this book I connected with the divine in meditation and then let the words come – a channelling of sorts. I believe that is why they seem to connect with so many people.

However, if there are any acrostics that don't speak to your healing, I encourage you with all my heart to rewrite them and to even write your own personal acrostics to deepen your experience. For example, perhaps your mother called you "Silly Sarah" or you had an abusive partner called "David" or you were attacked in "Malta" or ridiculed at "St Mary's Primary". You get the idea.

Throughout this book, my intention is to hold space for your healing and give prompts for your own inquiry and search. If you are triggered by any of the acrostics and the words in them, please take that as a sign to step towards your healing.

Sometimes we need to be woken up, and although it isn't my motivation, being triggered can sometimes be the beginning of a deep clearing for people. Please look at why you are feeling on high alert and breathe into the why with a view to taking the charge out of it and removing its power over you – that's what this book is about after all.

For this reason, and if the work calls you, I've written a three-layered clearing meditation at the end of the book. The effectiveness of a clearing meditation is not dependent on any kind of belief; you don't have to be a spiritual person to get huge benefit out of it. And furthermore, it can't hurt to try, so go ahead.

Finally, let this book be a gift to yourself, or to your beloveds. I believe that if she is in your hands now, it's for a reason. You are being called to action. When we commit to healing ourselves, we heal those around us; when we rise we lift, when we raise our vibration, up goes that of the universe.

So, thank you. We really do need you.

# RECLAIMING THE WORDS THAT HAVE HURT US

**WITCH**

**W**omxn's work:
**I**ntuitively and bravely
**T**eaching and guiding;
**C**onnecting to nature and
**H**ealing our collective wounds.

**TART**

Taught
At a young age to
Read lust as love and
To base self-esteem on sexual interest.

**BITCH**

Blindly
I
Took all your
Chaos into my
Heart. Until now.

**HARRIDAN**

Honestly, I'm just very
Angry
Right now, and I have every
Right to be
In light of all the
Dreams I've squashed for you,
And the rivers I've cried. I'm
Not as tough as I seem.

HIGH MAINTENANCE

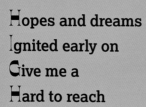

Hopes and dreams
Ignited early on
Give me a
Hard to reach

Moving target; I
Always feel
Insufficient and
Need
To control
Everything around me.
Nothing would please me more than to have your
Attention, and for you to notice my
Needs for once. But it seems you
Can't.
Expectation is killing my joy.

**DRAMA QUEEN**

**D**arling! I'm
**R**eleasing
**A**ll
**M**y extra energy.
**A**llow it! My

**Q**uest, like yours, is to
**U**nderstand myself,
**E**ase my worries,
**E**njoy my life, and it has
**N**othing to do with you.

**S**ure to find the kind of
**L**ove I deserve
**A**mongst all of those
**G**uys. No? No.

**W**illing to do
**A**lmost anything to bag a
**G**olden boy

**TOMBOY**

Trees.
Ode to all the trees, scraped knees,
Months outside until the last drop of sun.
Boy was it fun. Until I was ten.
Only then did I learn: I was not being a
Young lady and all I loved to do was wrong.

**FRIGID**

For the longest time I will
Regret letting you
Inside me.
Go away and leave me
In peace to heal and
Decide if I ever want sex again.

**FLIRT**

Fuck off and
Leave me alone.
I'm
Really tired of trying to be friendly, only
To get groped later on.

**DOG**

Do you see her, an hour, a day after you
Openly mocked her in public? She's still
Glaring in the mirror, hating herself. Happy?

**U**nfortunately, no, I didn't
**G**et Mama's
**L**ovely features; such a shame, as
**Y**ou say. Such a deep, deep shame.

**D**o not
**I**nvalidate my
**V**ery real need to be seen
**A**nd heard. Help me.

# GOLD DIGGER

Growing up we didn't have much
Of anything and I saw my parents
Labour through life until their
Dying day. I've worked hard since. I'm tired.

Diego proposed after three months.
It was too fast but I said yes!
Good god why shouldn't I? I'm not
Getting any younger. Do I love him? Look,
Every man I dated before him
Ran away when they heard I had kids.

**PRINCESS**

Pretty please don't show me the
Real world
In all its chaos.
No one believes I
Can handle myself,
Especially me. I'm denying
Sovereignty and power to
Save myself from the pain of being cast out.

**CRONE**

Connie overheard her grandson,
Robert, in the garden with his friends:
Oh, don't listen to her,
No one does. She's ancient.
Everyone thinks she's lost it.

**INSECURE**

I imagine I once felt invincible.
Now I often feel invisible.
Some say it comes with age: the
Ebbing away of
Confidence. No longer feeling as
Useful, as sexy, as
Radical. My wounded
Ego is tired. My soul waits patiently.

**THEY**

Trans and non-binary friends need allies.
Happy, free, respected and seen:
Everyone deserves that and
You already know how to use pronouns.

# HYSTERICAL

Hit her,
You know what I mean? A
Slap! Slap her face.
That's what you do. To calm her.
Everyone knows that!
Really. She's just being manipulative.
It used to be called female hysteria: one
Cure was to massage her genitals. It was
Associated with sorcery of course. Freud said
Lack of sex does it. She just needs a shag.

# BALL & CHAIN

Before we got married,
All you wanted to do was
Lie with your head in my
Lap

&

Claim me as yours.
Hard times and
Arguments have turned us
Into adversaries; and
No-one is winning here.

## OLD BAG

Oh it hurts; to no
Longer get the respect I
Deserve.

Back in the day I was quite the thing:
Attractive, articulate, alive. Don't worry, dear;
Granny just has something in her eye.

## FRUMP

Far from
Rejecting the
Urge to shine, I just don't believe I
Must conform to your
Personal ideal of femininity.

**BOMBSHELL**

Bombs are dangerous. Fragile. They go
Off. They destroy, they
Maim. Is my
Beauty that intimidating?
Surely you weren't scared of Miss Jean
Harlow? That sweet girl. Dead at twenty-six.
Engaged at sixteen.
Listen, I get it honey. All those pretty
Ladies scare you. So you weaponise them.

**COW**

Casually muttered under your breath
Over the meal I just
Wasted on a complete arsehole.

**HUSSY**

Honey, I shouldn't say, it's too
Ugly. But it's just
Such a
Shame the way that
Young girl conducts herself. Shameful.

**DRAGON**

During my years climbing the
Rungs
And working double your hours to bow myself in
Gratitude for your taking a chance on a womxn, I
Ought to have found an outlet for my
Near blind rage. But I didn't have time.

**NAG**

Not the first time I've
Asked you for
God's sake!

# TOO EMOTIONAL

Time and again we've
Opened up this position to the
Opposite sex and

Every bloody time we've
Massively regretted it. Right, guys?
Our experience is that you ladies
Tend to find
It challenging to keep a level head.
Oh yeah, the heart is important too but
No-one likes to see a woman go to pieces
All over the news room!
Let us guys write about the tough stuff, hey?

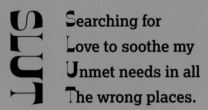

**S**earching for
**L**ove to soothe my
**U**nmet needs in all
**T**he wrong places.

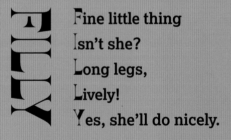

**F**ine little thing
**I**sn't she?
**L**ong legs,
**L**ively!
**Y**es, she'll do nicely.

# SLOANE RANGER

So much is assumed because my life looks so good.
Lord knows
Only Mummy
Actually asks if I'm okay.
Not that I would admit to
Everyone that I fucked up. Or that I hurt myself.

Running
Away and eloping
Never did appeal. But Jonno thinks big weddings are
God awful and
Everyone knows he's got great taste. I
Regret not having my sister there, though. Oh well.

## WENCH

**W**hen you pull me onto your lap
**E**very evening, your foul breath on my
**N**eck and your dirty-nailed fingers
**C**aressing flesh too firm for your too-old
**H**orrid hands. Yes, sir. On my way, sir.

## SHEILA

**S**he runs a good clean house and
**H**as my dinner ready
**E**very night at 5pm. I mean her sewing ain't
**I**deal! By no means. But she's a good
**L**ady you know? Doesn't make a fuss
**A**nd a great mum to the girls.

**E**veryone says we are all
**S**tupid and obsessed with
**S**ex and want to shop
**E**very minute of the day.
**X**tra gd at sxtng,

**G**iving head,
**I**nventing shit just to gossip about,
**R**adiate fake tan and
**L**iterally just there to look at.

**CATTY**

Could it be that the
Attitude you assign to me has something
To do with
The way
You belittle me?

**PIG**

Poor girl! But she doesn't help herself!
If I was that fat I would definitely
Go on a diet. Then they wouldn't tease her.

LIPSTICK LESBIAN

Literally every social event
Includes someone telling me I'm too
Pretty to be a lesbian.
So, I'm supposed to take
This as a compliment? You understand that this
Implies that other lesbians
Can be gay, to your mind, because they are ugly?
Kick yourself.

Let's get this straight for you (pun intended):
Even though I dress femme and have a
Sizeable shoe collection, I'm not
Biding my time until the right man comes along.
I'm not bisexual or trying something out,
And yes I know men think I am hot, but that means
Nothing to me. Truly. Seriously. Nothing.

## NEUROTIC

**N**ice to meet you, I have
**E**xtreme reactions to stress, I am an
**U**tter workaholic and
**R**aging perfectionist. Why? Trauma.
**O**h yes. Don't you worry, this
**T**ype A womxn, this terrified child/adult
**I**s acutely self-aware. But I can't stop. I live in
**C**onflict between my worries and life plan.

## COUGAR

**C**oming here was a mistake. I'm too
**O**ld. Half of them look
**U**nderage for
**G**od's sake. I could get
**A**rrested. Oh no thank you, I'm not drinking.
**R**eally, you think so? That's sweet of you.

**SKANK**

So you think I'm trash. Oooo …
Kaaaaay. You liked my scrawny
Ass last week and you kissed my greasy
Neck and liked my pockmarked chest. I
Know who I am. You don't see her.

**DIRTY**

Do me harder.
I love it like that.
Ride me baby.
Talk dirty to me.
Yes yes yes (oh god please no).

# PUSSYCAT

**P**ull up my skirt and pull down my

**U**nderwear.

**S**ee! I

**S**queal. I made her pretty for

**Y**ou. No more naughty

**C**urly hair down there!

**A**ren't I a good little kitty. Stroke my

**T**ummy. Make me purrrrrrrrrrrrrrr.

## CRAZY

Calling you out on your behaviour
Rather than
Accepting another billion
Zillion insults, slights and hurts from
You. Not crazy babe – just over my limit.

## SEX KITTEN

Scene one:
Even had flowers in my trailer!
XXX thank you for being part of this film.

Kind. So kind. Just one thing …
I don't see why she
Takes her
Top off in Scene five. She's washing her car?
Even though she's written as shy? Oh okay
Not that kind of shy. No problem! Topless is fine …

# TROLLOP

Tom said he loved me.

Rory had such a nice voice.

Ollie was so sophisticated.

Lennox said he wasn't that kind of guy.

Luke said: "Sssh it's okay baby just relax".

Olivia said I should just try it once and see.

People like to fuck me. Who am I to object?

**PORKER**

Please don't say it
Out loud. I will
Remove myself if you just leave me alone. I
Know I am disgusting. I think it
Every second of every day. I
Really want out of my body.

**TO**

Happy to eat me
Out and then slag me off.

## COCK TEASE

Could it actually be
Okay to
Celebrate one's sexiness
Knowing you want nothing more?

Talk to me; ask me; let's see if our
Expectations
Are the
Same. Then
Everyone is clear and in the clear.

## HARPY

Half-mythical creature
And half-grasping,
Roaring womxn.
Plumed unfashionably and being a
Yawning bore.

# VALLEY GIRL

Val dudes are the worst.
Ah! What's your damage?!
Lay a hand on me and I'll scream.
Lame. Taxiiiiiiiiiiiii … take me to
Errrrr, San Fernando Valley,
You freak.

Gag me with a spoon
I will barf on you if you make me wear last year's
Ralph Lauren. Daddy only notices new things.
Life is a lot about how I look next to him.

## PORNSTAR

Pumping in and
Out
Repeatedly;
Never checking if I am
Satisfied but you know,
Truth is he's
A good guy so I fake it. Loudly.
Really turns him on. One of us should be.

## MINGER

Mostly
I don't look in the mirror, I
Notice how other
Girls look and know I'm different; I see
Exactly how ugly I am by how you
React when I come near you.

## FEISTY

Fuck me if I want something
Enough to show passion for it.
I know you are intimidated by my
Sass but don't feel
Threatened;
You and I were never competing.

## MINX

Mum, he had his hand on my leg.
I did not encourage him!
No, I wasn't flirting with him! Mum,
Xav may be your friend, but he's also a dick.

**TIGER MOM**

Total focus on the
Intellect, drive, ambition and
Growth mindset of my offspring
Ensures that I do not get time to
Read books like yours, Amy Chua!

My own missed
Opportunities and broken dreams wait to
Meet me late at night. I take an Ambien.

**HONEYPOT**

How to love me without
Objectifying me?
No, I know you're trying to
Engage in cute banter.
Yes, the word sounds sweet but
Put another way it feels like
Ownership, reduction; like I'm a fruit
To be thrown away after being sucked.

**NASTY**

No I'm serious
A.F.
She'll let you do whatever
To her, bro!
Yeah, she's nasty.

# JAILBAIT

Just look how much she's grown.
Aren't you going to break hearts!
I bet you have all the boys
Lusting after you.
Big breasts like that on
A young girl.
If I was twenty years younger! Ha!
Tell you what, I'll give you a lift.

## THOT

That 'ho' over there
Has a heart, soul, immune system; she has
Opinions, dreams, wisdom, secrets …
Think that over before you open your mouth.

## LOLITA

Leer at me,
Ogle me,
Lick your lips.
I want you.
Tell me what you want to do to me.
And then take me home, please.

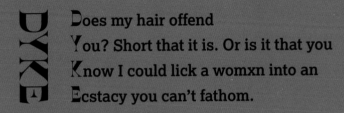

**DYKE**

Does my hair offend
You? Short that it is. Or is it that you
Know I could lick a womxn into an
Ecstacy you can't fathom.

**BOSSY**

Bitchy
Old me, having the audacity to
Suggest you get off your arse and
Sort your shit out so I don't have to cover for
You, yet again.

**TRANNY**

To whom said and spoken by whom? A
Reclamation and hard-won identity or
A shouted precursor to violent assault?
Now a celebration of queerness? Or a
Nasty slur intended to dehumanise?
You say. You decide. We're listening.

**VIXEN**

Vicky wasn't sure
If he meant, in a flirty way, that she was an
X-rated kind of lady, or if he was implying
Everyone thought she
Needed to stop wearing such low-cut tops.

**HOOKER**

Hjgh heels
On.
Own feelings off.
Kegels done for the day.
Everything waxed off.
Ready to fucking earn.

**ROUGH**

Ringing you just in case I was
Out and you called me at home.
Um, but you don't have my landline so
Good, okay. Last night was good. Did you
Have fun? I was surprised you liked— ...hello?

**SENSITIVE**

So many hurtful things. Felt deeply.
Eventually it was too much. But today I
Nestle in a creative, loving life. Yes, I am
Sensitive. Thank God I am. It's my magic.
I didn't always understand it was a gift; a child
That pleased in order to survive this world.
I feel deeply, think deeply, love deeply. I
Vow never to betray myself again;
Each breath is a reminder of my journey.

**HE-SHE**

Hello my name is
Ellen. If you

Stepped into my shoes for even
Half an hour you would
Ease up on the abuse. I've bled to be me.

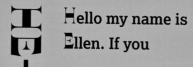

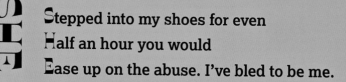

# WELFARE QUEEN

We always find someone to point our
Entitled white fingers at. Way back when
Linda Taylor was living high on tax payers' dollars,
Fur coats and Cadillacs
And without a care in the world,
Righteous Ronald Reagan decided the
Economy was the only thing that mattered.

Queens don't choose their start in life.
Under Reagan the ugly stereotyping
Emerged: moral rot, a Black inner-city
Endemic. Watch out! She's everywhere. A
New villainess to blame the economy on.

**BIMBO**

Beautiful daughter remember this:
In life you absolutely
Must not be too sexy, or they won't
Believe you're clever; but sexy enough,
Or else they won't even care.

**TIDY**

Take a step back.
I am not your instrument.
Don't touch me.
Your desire does not give you rights.

DIFFICULT

Dare you shame her? She

Is committed to getting it done. She

Fights her own corner and is

Fully prepared to be contrary.

Immovable, stubborn, determined:

Covetable characteristics in a strong man.

Understand, she knows what she's sacrificing.

Loving a difficult womxn is difficult. And

The path she's on requires her to be difficult. So she is.

**FIT**

Feels like
It's maybe a compliment but it's also
Totally sexually objectifying.

**MILF**

Maybe
I should
Learn to respect my
Fucking elders.

**BATTLE AXE**

Because I have
Asked you
To step out of your comfort zone;
To bring me something better; to
Let go of your
Ego and try it my way, you

Attack me, mock me,
X-ray my body with your
Eyes and make me an enemy.

# ARM CANDY

**A**vailable for wounded egos, the
**R**ecently divorced as well as
**M**arried folks and the

**C**olossally rich,
**A**s a
**N**od to your success and a
**D**istraction from the
**Y**outh you can't let go of.

## SOCCER MOM

Sure I drive a Toyota Avalon and shop at
Outlet stores. Yes, my staple outfit includes
Cargo shorts paired with
Cute cardigans and some comfortable slip-ons.
Everybody makes choices, and mine was to
Raise my babies in the suburbs.

Mock me if you will. Reduce me to a cliché but
Oh, you know nothing of my wild plans.
Mama's heart still beats for the big dreams.

**SKET**

See me for me.
Kiss me with love.
Everyone is lying. I didn't
Touch his dick. I'm sorry!

**CUNT**

Calm yourself …
Understand that your anger is
Not about me. But a
True reflection of you.

YUMMY MUMMY

You are
Undressing me with your
Mind whilst your dog sits on my lap,
My husband laughs at your joke and
Your wife pours me a much-needed

Martini.
Unbelievable.
Men aren't all like you, thank God, but
Many have eye-fucked a mummy they thought
Yummy. Most often in front of her kids.

**SEX WORKER**

Sex sells. And I sell my sex.
Everyone has bills. We are
X-rated service providers.

We are students, migrants, victims,
One-parent households, entrepreneurs; the
Recently let go, the full-time carers. We
Know the risks and stigma. We
Earn money for our families, futures, habits,
Rent; some like it. Some don't. Some pay tax.

**MUNTER**

Maybe
Underneath my
Not-good-enough-for-society face,
Tits, bum and legs
Everything else is actually more important. I
Realised today that I'm perfectly imperfect.

# TROUBLE & STRIFE

Tell you what,
Rob. Try a bit of time
On your own.
Understand I love you
But this
Life is less than I
Ever expected

&

Something needs
To change.
Rachel needs to be up at seven
In time for the bus. Tell her I'm at Mum's.
Find something in the freezer to
Eat for dinner. Bye, Rob.

**WHORE**

When you use my body to
Hold your desires, disappointments,
Orgasms and needs, but
Reject me after you've taken my
Energy because you now feel like shit.

**PLASTIC**

Pretty decent face but
Lies
About so much
Shit.
Totally fake.
I think she's insecure.
Can't be arsed with the drama.

**OLD LADY**

Oh don't worry,
Love. I
Don't give a shit what

Lads of sixteen think of me.
At home my
Darling wife of thirty
Years is stirring my Martini.

# ASKING FOR IT

Am I the reason it happened?
Should I report it to my boss? I'm
Kicking myself for wearing that skirt.
I don't want to get fired. I
Need this job.  Be one of the
Guys they said; show some leg and

Find the salty jokes hilarious
Or you'll go nowhere fast.
Rape. Harassment. Just a kiss.

I don't care if you like me, just
That you believe me. I didn't want it.

## FILTHY

Funny how it was you who encouraged her to
Imitate the womxn in the porn you watch
Long into
The night. And now you describe
Her to
Your work mates as filthy.

## SIREN

Sisters gathered
In watery clusters,
Rising together in a song
Every human yearns for and
No-one ever remembers the next morning.

THINKING MAN'S CRUMPET

To be offended or not?
How does
It sit with me? I
Notice a sort of awkward smile
Kiss my lips and
Instead of really going there I
Nod and take the "compliment". For
God's sake Joan Bakewell didn't

Mind. It seems
A bit ludicrous if I
Natter on about it!
'
Still, I do feel a little bit

Cornered, if that makes sense. Or
Rather, labelled for retail.
Understand me though, I'm aware of
My
Privilege. Not
Every one is both intelligent and beautiful.
TV and radio lie ahead for me no doubt.

## STUPID

Seeing you now as I do, it
Takes a moment to truly
Understand and honour how
Painful this word once was to you.
I see only a goddess. Who
Dared to try to diminish you? Fool.

## SEXY

Sending an
Echo down my timeline:
X O X O, teenage me.
You are much, much more than this.

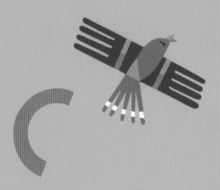

**WOMXN**

**W**onder about us?
**O**ut here, looking up,
**M**aking it work under the
**X**-ray scrutiny and pressures
**N**o human can live up to.

THIS IS
YOUR HEALING

# DEEPER WORK

Welcome to the deeper work. By now you've probably found a good handful of words that have triggered you or stirred something within you. Here is where we clear the pain, rinse out the poison and take the sting clean out.

Everything we do begins as a thought, an instinct or a vibration of energy within our system. Every action, every word, every human creation exists first in our imagination or consciousness. If you can conceive of it, it can exist. If you can picture it, you can also bring it into reality. Your brain cannot differentiate perfectly between what is real and what is a creation of the mind. In simple terms, your brain believes your mental action and your real actions are the same. Huge amounts of research have been done, proving that even if you are sitting down in rest, thinking about an action will fire the same neural pathways in your brain as if you were actually doing it! With that understanding you can now see the huge potential that visualisation techniques, like the ones used in the following clearing meditaion, can have. The emotions that we have embodied can be physically, mentally and spiritually cleared from your body, all from the comfort of your home.

The clearing meditation I have written is in the form of a reading visualisation, which means that sometimes you will be reading what comes next and sometimes you will be encouraged or will feel drawn to close your eyes to visualise a part of the journey, or to leave reality and to venture inside your mind. Let that be a fluid thing and intuitive; there is no right or wrong. If you do find yourself closing your eyes, just open them again when you are ready for the next part.

You may not get through the whole thing. It may take you a week of doing a bit daily, or you may do it four times in a row. It's all perfect. Feel free to also record yourself reading it, on your phone or computer and play it back to yourself.

I have used BITCH here as an example but please substitute that word with whichever one you are working on that day. This is a continuous journey in deep progress and the more you practice, the more you will shift and the greater the benefits will be. Go at your own pace and trust your subconscious mind and your higher self. They've got your back.

# A CLEARING MEDITATION

## BEGINNING THE HEALING

Come to stillness in the place where you are. This is your healing.

Set the intention to clear all hurt, heaviness, pain, trigger and potency from the word BITCH, through all time, space, dimension and reality.

> Say the word to yourself several times, either in your head or out loud.
>
> *Where do you feel that word strike you? In what part of your body?*

If the word BITCH had a colour, what would it be? And if the word BITCH had a shape what would it be?

> Nothing has to make sense here, nothing is right or wrong. Just let the first answers come up to the surface.
>
> *For example, BITCH could be a heavy red disc that thumps in your head but strikes you in your heart, or it could be a blue bowtie that feels like a lump in your throat – that sort of thing. The more specific you can get, the better.*

Notice if you are holding your breath, and, if you are, relax and then exhale.

You are shifting. You are clearing. This is safe. You are safe.

This is okay. You will only go as far into this as you can handle.

Now you can begin the healing.

What colour could you bring in, pull down and absorb that could lift and lighten, clear and shift the word, colour, shape and weight of BITCH in your physical body?

*For a moment, before you continue, close your eyes and imagine the colour you've chosen pouring down onto you from above. It streams down onto the top of your head and flows directly to the area of your body that feels the word most – it could be your head, throat, chest or anywhere else.*

Allow that colour to do its work in that area.

Take your time.

Wait until you turn the red disc or the blue bowtie – or whatever shape the word BITCH has taken – to your chosen colour.

Next, let your colour flow down all over your skin. It washes down over every part of you that exists. Visualise that now, all the way down to your feet.

*If you feel any resistance anywhere, just bring your attention to that place, lovingly knowing that it needs a little more coaxing to shift, and just bring in more of your chosen colour.*

Now, send that colour inside you, into all your organs, bones, blood and cells so that your whole body is reverberating with it at the same time. You will get very good at this with practice. When you have filled your inner and outer body to the fullest it can be, check in with yourself.

Do you feel you have shifted?

*If not, take a breather – sometimes shifts will happen a few hours or days later. But if you feel drawn to, you can repeat this part of the visualisation – just start again.*

However, if you have shifted in your present moment, now it is time to check whether you need to clear this word from your past.

## CLEARING THE PAST

Imagine the timeline of your life.

See it in your mind's eye stretching out so you can see your entire life in full.

*Maybe some particular memories jump out, maybe they don't. Maybe it's hard to visualise – that's okay. Just hold the idea; that's enough for this to work.*

Now bring back to mind the colour you chose to clear, lift and lighten the word BITCH. Pull that colour down once more from above, filling every cell and feeling the vibration of that colour and energy in your heart centre.

Now we are going to send that colour directly through your heart and all the way down your timeline. Set the intention that it will go to all the places where you needed healing in the past – all of the times you needed to feel safe, heard, respected, loved, encouraged, and were not.

*Take some time to do this. Allow images, memories, faces, words and thoughts to come up, and as they do, frame them with your chosen colour and let it seep into every corner of the picture/thought in your mind.*

If nothing comes up, do not worry; continue to see the timeline in your mind and keep sending your colour towards and down it until the whole timeline is that colour.

If you find yourself coming in and out of the visualisation, questioning the process, or if you feel it's not working for you, just come back to feeling your heart beating in your chest and relax, knowing that you are taking exactly what you need from this, and – whether you believe in the process or not – it is working on and with you.

If a particular person comes strongly into your thoughts, whether you feel you can forgive them or not, simply imagine sending them that colour. This is not a gift for them, it is a gift for you. Forgiveness doesn't mean that you weren't wronged, it doesn't deny your pain, it doesn't let anyone off the hook. Oh no. Forgiveness sets YOU free. When you no longer hold hate, anger or grief in your heart generated by the past with that person, they no longer have an energetic hold over you, and you have moved on without them. They can never touch you again. It is a process, and everyone moves towards forgiveness at their own perfect pace. Don't rush yourself, just send them that colour, keep practicing and set your sights on freedom.

So, how far back down your timeline did you go? To your child-self, baby-self, foetus-in-the-womb-self? If not, send your chosen colour all the way back there now, too.

See your foetus-self floating around in your mother's womb and fill that womb with colour so you are swimming in it. Let your tiny self absorb all this fluid colour.

*Remember to keep breathing deeply, noting and observing what comes up, but letting it pass along.*

## GOING BEYOND THE PAST

And what if we now went further? Let us go back to a past life. Whether you believe in reincarnation, other dimensions in non-linear time, the power of story and imagination or nothing at all. It doesn't matter, it will work regardless.

Close your eyes for a moment and breathe a little deeper, sinking a little lower into the place your body is resting. Bring the word BITCH back towards you. Feel and see its power and its hold.

Now, if you knew of a past-life that felt that way, that held the same energy as that feeling, where would you go to see it? Don't question it and don't dissect it – not now, just go with it.

Now imagine you are transporting yourself there. You will be safe, you are protected. You can go there and you will not be harmed further. We are observers this time around. We are our own healers.

Imagine yourself arrived. In your mind's eye look down at your feet.

*What do they look like? Are you wearing shoes, boots or are you barefoot? Are your feet in grass, sand, mud, on concrete, carpet or something else?*

When you can see or imagine your feet, observe the rest of you.

*Who are you? Let a name come to mind. You may be a different gender, age, race, height or speak another language. Solidify this reality by noticing everything you are wearing.*

Take your time.

Now lift your head and look around. Where are you?

*Describe it to yourself. Out loud or in your head. Do you know what year it is? Let a date just fly in. Keep flowing with this work; don't doubt it or question it right now. Whether we call it past-life work or mere imagination, the healing will be the same.*

Before investigating further, pull down a bubble of protective white light to cover you so that you feel safe. Let it settle over you. Take a deep breath and feel the white light fit tightly and comfortably around your body.

Now you are protected and you are free to open up to why you are here. Ask yourself: what happened to me here? What am

I here to see? Maybe your feet start walking and take you to something you need to see. Maybe you are exactly where you need to be already. Let it unfold. See and recognise what you are here to observe and heal.

*It helps to keep sensing your surroundings. What can you smell, see, hear, feel under your feet or reach to touch? If you are pulled straight into a story then run with it. Let it happen, and watch knowing you are safe.*

It may be emotional to witness or it may feel distant. It's all good – there is no right way. Take your time.

You may find no particular scene unfolding, in which case, just be in the atmosphere of it all.

*What colours do you notice?*

If at any point you feel overwhelmed, simply open your eyes, take a few deep breaths with your hand on your heart, and come back into the room. You can step back into the meditation again when you are ready or at a later date.

If you are choosing to carry on, start to send your chosen healing colour from your heart space and out into this world you find yourself in. Let it just flow out of your heart and go where it needs to, DO what it needs to.

Feel the colour coming through you. It is a powerful energy, divine, if you like. Trust that it knows what to do. You just need to channel it.

*Whilst that colour does its work, ask yourself: is there anything I need to resolve here? Anything I need to change? Should I intervene? Offer advice? Change the course of this story? Help someone? If the answer is yes then follow that impulse and let it unfold. Take your time.*

When you feel all here is complete, and if it feels like the necessary resolution has been met – or if you are just done – say goodbye to the people/creatures/plants/beings/energies you have connected with, and/or to the place you are in. Let them know you can return here if needed. They can simply call you.

Now go back to where you first landed in this world or time. From that place look back towards it all and imagine taking a step away, as if the world gets smaller when you step back. See it as a snapshot – a picture that you are looking at, hanging up in front of you.

*Imagine encompassing that picture in a beautiful picture frame made with the healing colour you have been working with. Be specific with how the frame looks. Modern? Ornate? Simple? Detailed? See your chosen colour in it. This frame will continue to hold your story and your healing long after you have finished the visualisation and, perhaps, always. You have shifted a great deal whether it feels like it in this moment or not.*

Come away and back into your body now. Start to become aware of the heartbeat in your chest, the blood in your veins, your breath. Feel the air on your skin and the points of contact your body has with the chair or bed or surface you are on. Sink back into your brilliant body and into the current time and space. Slowly start to move, as it feels good to. If you find your eyes closing as you complete this last part of the meditation, open them now, stretch out and move.

Then come back to stillness. Notice what feels different, what feels familiar. Take three deep breaths, closing your eyes again if you wish. In through the nose and out through the nose – 1 … 2 … 3 …

Come back fully now. And when it feels right, open your eyes.

Welcome back. Congratulate yourself – you have changed your life.

## IN THE COMING DAYS

Over the next few days notice what feels new. Shifts can continue in the minutes, hours, days and weeks after. You are clearing old patterns, stuck energy and past wounds. You will not shift any faster than you can handle. This is not new energy; you have been holding it for a long time. What will be new is the space it leaves when the old energy completely clears. We want to fill that space with energy that pulls you towards your best life, your true purpose, your highest calling, your deepest healing.

Each time you use this guided visualisation to clear a word or energy, spend the next few days infusing your life with the colour you chose for the healing. I recommend that my clients buy themselves flowers of that colour, wear clothes they have of that colour, paint a picture using only or predominantly that colour, do a collage of that colour or simply sit and imagine that colour flowing into their body during quiet moments.

The more you use your healing colour, the deeper the benefits. And you will want to; as soon as you start to feel the beauty and power of colour in your life, you will keep returning to it. It is available to all. It need cost nothing. And, best of all, you can spread it to others. Imagine sending a deep-pink rose to a friend or buying your aunt a light-blue scarf; make a dark-green salad for your partner when she is overwhelmed at work or wrap your child in an orange blanket when they need soothing.  The psychology of colour is fascinating, but the healing power of colour is utterly magical.

# LEXY

Lexy Wren-Sillevis (she/her) is a therapist, healer and respected energy psychologist. She is also just that person that people open up and pour their hearts out to (and recognises that as a privilege).

This book is the culmination of almost a decade of spiritual work and therapy with private clients; and a lifetime of being a womxn occasionally called awful names.

Lexy has always worked with words, and is a wordsmith and storyteller at heart. She studied journalism at Cardiff University before working for the very first online magazine, BeMe.com, and has since written articles for *Hip & Healthy* and *The Numinous*. She also taught Shakespeare to 6–22-year-olds on behalf of the RSC for two years.

Lexy lives in London with her husband, two daughters, their cat Kurt Russell, and Claude their miniature dachshund.

# MARGAUX

Margaux Carpentier is an image maker and storyteller. She creates pictures using a symbolic language, so each piece can be read by all, in many different ways.

Her work records the infinite combinations of colours offered by the world and her images transcribe the choreography of living things.

She works on varied projects, from large murals, installations and paintings to detailed book illustrations, and even toys.

Margaux was born in France and has been living in the UK for 12 years. What inspires her above all are the books she reads, her walks in the old, overgrown cemetery (and when life allows it, elsewhere in the world), and conversations at the pub with the people she loves; or strangers.

## WORKING ON THIS BOOK

Something I enjoy about drawing pictures is to set them free as soon as I feel them finished. I like to make them unspecific yet precise, to leave clues. I use shapes, symbols and colours like a storyteller or a poet would use words.

Working on this book was a dream of an experience. I got to work from words, arguably my first source of inspiration, and Lexy's raw words felt perfect. They pushed me to explore new themes and emotions.

Hopefully our words and images will resonate with every womxn's experience and make us stronger together.

**ACKNOWLEDGEMENTS**

First and foremost, I want to thank all of you for choosing *Womxn: Sticks & Stones* when there are so many incredible books out there. You are absolutely amazing, you are part of The Light Work and I hope you feel better for having this book in your life. You are raising the vibration. You are spreading the healing. Thank you.

I also want to place here, a reiteration of my true belief that these words came from a higher version of myself.

So, thank you the DIVINE. You work FAST!

Back on earthly terms I want to thank my publisher Lucy Pessell for being the force behind *Sticks & Stones* and the designer of the beautiful innards. Having someone truly understand your vision is a rare thing and I will never take our connection, your humour or your hard work for granted. Thank you for believing.

Next to my editor Sarah, you are so easy to work with, so clever and hold such a clear vision for this book. You have added hugely to all the words. It's been an utter pleasure. Thank you.

To Hannah for her fantastic eye and brilliant choices and for being a superb go-between.

To Evi O studio, for her genius, genius cover.

To Margaux for the deeply healing colours and for your nuance and brilliance. You are a real creatrix and hold such a high vision of true equality for all which I deeply honour and echo. One of my top life moments was you agreeing to illustrate this book! Thank you. Thank you. Thank you.

To the womxn in my life: the most inspiring and special. I wish we spent more time together – I'm terrible at reaching out (I'm working on it! my next acrostic for myself will be BURDEN): Marisa, Pascale, Lily, Ruby, Hannah, Bex, Laura H, Scarlett, Amy, Fran, Rhiannon, Emma, Becca, Goldie, Occy, Mell, Ali, Camilla, Lucy, Leisha, Laura L, Brandei, Sura, Elena, Jo, Jess, Kelly, Amara, Sarah, Sam, Katy, Nicola – you are my circle: my constant source of inspiration and a deep pleasure in my life. From near or far, recent friends or from very far back in my life – you are my womxn. Thank you.

To Kate for being an inspiration not only to our Marley but to me and many other womxn too: for marching and protesting and creating and believing in better (and for keeping contact when you didn't have to). I wish you blue skies always.

To Anneke, for opening your heart and home to both my daughters equally. I will never be able to express what that means. For all the talks and walks, thank you.

To all my aunts and womxn cousins. What a tribe we are! Huge thanks for all your love and lessons. To my Auntie Carry, thank you for being such a warm light in my life.

To Korani and Katherine, to Victoria and Lucy (and of course to Melissie, our brave rainbow Queen) – you are my colour sisters. My teachers. I love you. You are who I turn to in my life moments. The journey is less lonely and more beautiful alongside you. Thank you with all my heart.

To Sharon King, for being the first to show me how to step into and clear past lives. Many people have benefited from your teaching. Thank you.

To Hermine, for co-creating Len.

To my Gagamama Amanda, you taught me about feminism, you showed me what we need to do, with humour and sass and class and flair. I love you.

To my Grandmére Joan, and my Nana Betty for being strong women in very different, equally phenomenal ways.

To my mother Sally, for teaching me many lessons. Our relationship has not always been easy but you have always loved me deeply and supported me with all you have to give. I learned about saints, angels, Jesus, God and especially Mary from you; the preciousness of that is profound. I love you. Thank you.

And to Lenny (and his karaoke alter ego Gabby), the only man on this list – I love you. Thank you for being the first person to read every one of these acrostics and for believing in their importance from the very beginning.